THE
TOTALLY
LEMONS
COOKBOOK

D0011760

THE
TOTALLY
LEMONS
COOKBOOK

By Helene Siegel & Karen Gillingham

Illustrated by Carolyn Vibbert

CELESTIAL ARTS
BERKELEY, CALIFORNIA

Copyright © 1999 by Helene Siegel and Karen Gillingham.

Illustrations copyright © 1999 by Carolyn Vibbert.
All rights reserved. No part of this book may be reproduced or transmitted in any form or by any means, electronic or mechanical, including photocopying, recording, or by any information storage and retrieval system without permission in writing.

The Totally Lemons Cookbook is produced by becker&mayer!, Ltd.

Printed in Singapore.

Cover design and illustration: Bob Greisen
Interior design and typesetting: Susan Hernday
Interior illustrations: Carolyn Vibbert

Library of Congress Cataloging-in-Publication Data
Siegel, Helene.

   The Totally lemons cookbook / by Helene Siegel and Karen Gillingham.

     p.   cm.

  ISBN 0-89087-887-0 (alk. paper)

  1. Cookery (Lemons) I. Gillingham, Karen. II. Title.
TX813.L4S54 1998
641.6'4334—dc21   98-37195

                                               CIP

Celestial Arts Publishing
P.O. Box 7123
Berkeley, CA 94707

Look for all 28 *Totally* books at your local store!

To lemon lovers everywhere

CONTENTS

INTRODUCTION

I t's easy to take lemons for granted. They are inexpensive, available all year round, and they keep well.

In addition, the lemon is a fruit that doesn't "behave" like a fruit. Unlike a good apple, a lemon can't be eaten out of hand or packed in a lunch box for a healthy treat. Nobody pines for a perfect lemon. And yet, just try living without them.

To the good cook, they are as essential as salt and pepper. Their juice adds vim and vigor to raw shellfish, smoked fish, and salads. Heavily spiced or rich stews and soups are brought into balance by a final squirt of lemon. Almost all fruits taste better seasoned with lemon juice. Tea, coffee, and mixed drinks come to life with a twist of lemon. And the lemon wedge is the low-fat cook's universal response to pallid chicken breasts, fish fillets, and steamed veggies.

Since nobody needs a recipe to add a squirt of lemon at the end of preparing a dish, we made it our job to assemble a group of great recipes with lemon as a featured flavor. From classic lemon bars, lemon poppy seed muffins, and marmalade to lemon pepper game hens, raw artichoke salad, and pasta with lemon cream sauce, the sour taste of lemon is integral to each dish.

Nothing says "sunshine" in the kitchen like a lemon. Its color and fragrance lift our spirits before we even taste it. (Legend says that the taste memory of lemon is so strong that the sight of someone sucking a lemon is enough to cause a pucker in those watching.) Household cleansers are often lemon-scented because lemons conjure freshness in ways an orange or lime never could.

So if life must mean taking the bitter with the sweet, we promise not to complain. As long as we've got lemons.

The thin yellow membrane covering the lemon is the zest. It contains the fragrant oils that deliver the most intense lemon flavor. Unlike the flavor of juice, which gets cooked away with heat, the flavor of zest lingers. Wash lemons well before zesting, and if a recipe calls for both zest and juice, always zest first. Once the zest is removed, store lemons in the refrigerator for later use.

The quickest way to remove zest is to rub the lemon against a grater. If you need longer threads, use a special zester made to obtain them. A shortcut for baking recipes in which zest and sugar are both called for is to remove the zest in pieces with a vegetable peeler or paring knife. Place in food processor along with sugar, and process until fine. Add to recipe when sugar is called for.

TANGY SOUPS,
SALADS,
AND
STARTERS

ARTICHOKE FENNEL SALAD

Look for small, delicate baby artichokes in the spring and summer in farmer's markets and well-stocked produce sections. Once baby artichokes are trimmed, the whole choke may be eaten.

juice of 1 lemon for soaking
20 baby artichokes
1 medium fennel bulb, trimmed
3 tablespoons lemon juice
6 tablespoons olive oil
2 tablespoons chopped fresh Italian parsley
salt and freshly ground pepper
4-ounce Parmesan cheese wedge

When life gives you lemons, make lemonade.
        —Anonymous

Have ready a large bowl of cold water mixed with the juice of one lemon. Trim artichoke stems and remove outer leaves until remaining inner leaves are pale and thin. Trim off top ¼ inch. With a sharp knife, cut each into 8 or 10 tiny wedges. Soak wedges in lemon water.

Cut fennel bulb in half lengthwise, and then thinly slice across width. Transfer to mixing bowl. Strain artichokes and add to fennel.

In another small bowl, whisk together lemon juice, olive oil, parsley, salt, and pepper. Pour over salad and toss well. Chill until serving time.

To serve, mound the salad on six serving plates. Thinly slice the Parmesan (shave with a cheese slicer if possible) and top each salad with Parmesan shavings. Serve cold.

SERVES 6

SOPA DE LIMÓN

This tart chicken soup is typical of the Yucatan region of southern Mexico.

2 tomatoes
1 small onion, with skin
1 serrano chile
3 garlic cloves, with skins
1 tablespoon vegetable oil
1 teaspoon ground cumin
1 quart chicken stock
1 cinnamon stick
1 lemon, thinly sliced
fried tortilla strips, avocado strips, minced onion, chopped cilantro, lemon wedges for garnish

Preheat the broiler. Place the tomatoes, onion, chile, and garlic on foil-lined tray. Place under broiler and cook, turning frequently, until charred all over. Let cool.

Remove skins of the tomatoes, onion, chile, and garlic. Remove chile seeds, if desired. Place all in blender, and purée until smooth.

Heat the oil in a large, heavy pot over medium-high heat. Pour in purée and cumin, and let bubble about 5 minutes. Pour in chicken stock and cinnamon stick. Bring to a boil, reduce to a simmer, and cook 30 minutes. Skim and discard foam and cinnamon stick. Add lemon slices and gently cook 10 minutes longer. Ladle into bowls and serve with garnishes to add at the table.

SERVES 4

LEMON-MARINATED SCALLOPS

Raw scallops marinated in a simple lemon and olive oil dressing start a meal with a sophisticated touch.

½ pound sea scallops
1 tablespoon lemon juice
2 tablespoons extra virgin olive oil
2 tablespoons minced chives *or* scallions
salt and freshly ground pepper
4 cups mixed salad greens

Rinse and pat dry the scallops. Thinly slice across width into about four pieces each and place in glass or ceramic bowl.

In a small bowl, whisk together lemon juice, oil, and chives or scallions. Season to taste with salt and pepper. Pour dressing over scallops and toss to coat evenly. Cover and chill 15 to 30 minutes. To serve, divide the salad greens on four serving plates. Mound the cold scallops over the top and serve.

SERVES 4

LEMON TAPENADE

This lusty olive spread from southern France is a terrific accompaniment to cocktails. Substitute California black olives or omit the anchovies for a less tangy spread.

1 (9.5-ounce) jar pitted Kalamata olives, drained
2 garlic cloves, roughly chopped
1 to 2 anchovy fillets
2 tablespoons capers
grated zest of 2 lemons
juice of 1 lemon
3 tablespoons olive oil
crackers *or* toasted baguette slices

In food processor or blender, combine olives, garlic, anchovies, capers, lemon zest, and juice. Pulse until finely chopped. With the machine running, slowly add oil until a chunky paste forms. Serve as a spread for crackers or bread. Store in the refrigerator.

MAKES ¾ CUP

GREEK EGG AND LEMON SOUP

This traditional Greek soup, avgolemono, *is a great dish to make when the cupboard is relatively bare and you have a comfort-food craving.*

5 cups chicken broth
½ cup long-grain rice
3 egg yolks
⅓ cup lemon juice
salt and freshly ground pepper

Bring the chicken broth to a boil in a medium saucepan. Stir in the rice, reduce the heat to medium-low, and cook, uncovered, about 20 minutes.

Meanwhile, in a small bowl, whisk the egg yolks until foamy. Slowly drizzle in lemon juice, whisking continuously. Ladle about 1 cup hot broth into egg mixture, whisking constantly. Remove saucepan from heat and stir in egg-broth mixture. Adjust salt and pepper to taste and serve hot. (Be careful not to bring to a boil.)

SERVES 4

MARINATED GARLIC SHRIMP

Boiling the shrimp in their shells retains more moistness and flavor.

2 pounds extra large shrimp in the shell
1 cup pitted Kalamata olives
½ cup lemon juice
8 garlic cloves, minced
3 tablespoons chopped fresh oregano *or* parsley
½ cup olive oil
salt and freshly ground pepper

Bring a large pot of salted water to a boil. Cook shrimp until bright orange, about 2 minutes, and drain. Let cool, peel, and slice in half lengthwise. Combine shrimp in large bowl with olives.

In a small bowl, whisk together lemon juice, garlic, oregano or parsley, oil, salt, and pepper. Pour over the shrimp mixture, toss well, and adjust with salt and pepper. Chill up to a day, stirring and tossing occasionally.

SERVES 8 TO 12

WATERCRESS AND AVOCADO SALAD WITH LEMON PEPPER DRESSING

The tartness of watercress and lemons is offset by avocado in this summertime favorite. Use it to accompany spicy grilled or roasted meats.

4 bunches watercress, trimmed
2 ripe avocados, peeled, pitted, and sliced
2 tablespoons lemon juice
6 tablespoons olive oil
salt
$\frac{1}{4}$ teaspoon cracked black pepper

Combine the watercress and avocados in a large bowl. Lightly toss.

In a small bowl, whisk together lemon juice, olive oil, salt, and pepper. Pour over salad, toss to coat evenly, and serve.

SERVES 4

LEMON-DRENCHED ENTRÉES

GRILLED GAME HENS
WITH LEMON PEPPER MARINADE

*Serve these tart, little game hens with some good
salsa and slices of rustic country bread toasted on
the grill.*

4 small game hens, about 12 ounces each,
    giblets removed
1 cup olive oil
1 tablespoon salt
1 tablespoon cracked black pepper
½ cup lemon juice
2 cups roughly chopped fresh herbs such as
    parsley, mint, oregano, basil
salt
additional herb sprigs and lemon wedges
    for garnish

Wash and pat dry the hens. Split in half lengthwise, removing excess skin and bone.

Whisk together the olive oil, salt, pepper, lemon juice, and herbs in a large shallow pan. Add hens, turning to coat evenly. Cover with plastic wrap and refrigerate 4 hours to overnight.

To cook, preheat the grill or broiler. Cook, skin-side toward the flame first, 12 minutes per side. Season with salt to taste. To serve, arrange on platter with lemon wedges and herbs as garnish.

SERVES 4

Cooking with Lemon

When adding lemon juice to a sauce or soup, for freshest flavor it is best to stir the juice in toward the end of cooking. In baking, lemon zest imparts the best lemon flavor when added with the liquid or fat ingredients. A recent product to appear on the market is lemon oil—a good quick substitute for zest. Use it sparingly since the flavor is quite intense.

SWORDFISH LEMON SKEWERS

To prevent splintering, soak wooden skewers in water for 15 minutes and then store in the freezer.

½ cup olive oil
½ cup lemon juice
1 teaspoon cracked black pepper
½ cup chopped fresh oregano
2 pounds swordfish, about 1½ inches thick
3 bell peppers, red, yellow, or green, seeded and
    cut in 1-inch squares
½ red onion, cut in 3 wedges
3 small lemons, cut in 4 wedges each
salt

In a glass or ceramic pan, whisk together olive oil, lemon juice, pepper, and oregano. Remove the skin, cut swordfish into 1½-inch cubes, and add to marinade. Toss to coat evenly, cover with plastic, and chill ½ hour.

Preheat the grill or broiler and brush the grate with oil.

Assemble the skewers by alternating fish with each type of pepper. Separate the onion layers and place one in the center of each skewer. Anchor each skewer at both ends with a lemon wedge. Season all over with salt, and brush with marinade.

Cook, turning frequently, until the fish is opaque and the vegetables charred on the edges, about 10 minutes total.

Serves 6

LINGUINE WITH LEMON CREAM SAUCE

This simple but delicious pasta is a specialty of Sicily, where lemons are a key crop.

  2 tablespoons butter
  3 lemons, zested in threads and juiced
  ¾ cup heavy cream
  1 tablespoon minced fresh mint
  salt and freshly ground pepper
  1 pound linguine *or* spaghetti, cooked and
     drained
  ½ cup grated Parmesan cheese and extra for
     sprinkling

Melt the butter in a large skillet over medium-low heat. Add the lemon zest threads and juice, and boil about 2 minutes. Reduce heat to low, add cream and mint, and cook 5 to 8 minutes to blend flavors and thicken slightly. Season generously with salt and pepper.

Place hot pasta in serving bowl. Top with sauce and ½ cup Parmesan. Toss well and serve hot with additional Parmesan.

SERVES 4

The Italian Lemon

Though Sicily is one of the world's largest producers of lemons, the lemon was actually a rarity in ancient Rome. It only appears in the mosaics of the very wealthy. Much later, lemons were cultivated in the colder north, at the famous lemon pavilions of Lake Garda, which were glass-enclosed hothouses protected by the surrounding mountains and lake.

GRILLED VEAL CHOPS GREMOLATA

Gremolata, a seasoning paste of lemon zest, garlic, and parsley, is the traditional accompaniment to braised veal shanks, or osso bucco. It also does an excellent job of jazzing up grilled chops.

8 sprigs rosemary
4 garlic cloves, flattened
4 veal loin chops
olive oil to cover
salt to taste

GREMOLATA

2 teaspoons grated and chopped lemon zest
2 garlic cloves, minced
1 tablespoon lemon juice
3 tablespoons extra virgin olive oil
$\frac{1}{4}$ teaspoon salt
freshly ground pepper to taste

Arrange the garlic and four rosemary sprigs in a small roasting pan. Place the chops on top and place another sprig of rosemary over each chop. Pour on olive oil to cover. Cover with plastic and marinate in the refrigerator 8 to 24 hours.

Preheat the grill or broiler. Remove chops and wipe off excess oil. Arrange on rack, and grill or broil the chops, about 6 minutes per side. Season with salt. Serve hot with a spoonful of gremolata on top.

To make the gremolata, combine the ingredients in a bowl and mix. Adjust seasonings with salt and pepper, and store in the refrigerator if not serving immediately.

SERVES 4

ROASTED WHITEFISH
WITH LEMON BUTTER

Delicate, fresh fish is best served simply. Make this a meal by spreading the lemon butter on toasted baguette slices and adding a spoonful to the evening's vegetables.

1½ pounds whitefish fillet, skin on
salt and freshly ground pepper
½ stick butter, softened
1 tablespoon chopped fresh parsley leaves
2 teaspoons grated lemon zest
1 teaspoon lemon juice
2 tablespoons olive oil

The French Lemon

Recognizing the importance of a cold glass of lemonade on a hot afternoon, the French government in 1676 created the official guild of lemonade makers called the Compagnie des Limonadiers. Vendors were licensed to sell their wares on the streets of Paris along with the coffee and chocolate sellers. At today's Parisian cafes

Preheat the oven to 350 degrees F. Cut fish
into four servings and season all over with salt and
pepper.

Beat together the butter, parsley, lemon zest,
and juice. Transfer to a small bowl and chill.

Heat the oil in a large ovenproof, nonstick skillet over high heat. Sauté the fish skin-side down,
until skin is crisp and golden, about
5 minutes. Turn the fish over and top each with a
tablespoon of lemon butter. Place skillet in oven
and roast 5 minutes longer. With a spatula, transfer fish to serving plates. Serve hot.

SERVES 4

the tradition continues in the citron presse—*a drink of
straight lemon juice served with a carafe of cold water, ice
cubes, and sugar to be added according to taste. During
the 18th century, considered the golden age of horticulture
in France, Louis XIV's gardener Le Notre planted 3,000
lemon trees in L'Orangerie, the garden at Versailles.*

ROAST LEMON CHICKEN

Lemon, garlic, and rosemary are a traditional Italian combination for roasted chicken.

1 (4-pound) roasting chicken
salt and freshly ground pepper
2 lemons
4 garlic cloves, crushed and peeled
3 sprigs rosemary
olive oil for drizzling

Preheat the oven to 425 degrees F.

Rinse the chicken inside and out. Generously season the cavity with salt and pepper. Cut one lemon in half across the width and cut the other into 16 wedges. Stuff the cavity loosely with one lemon half (halved again if too large), garlic, and two rosemary sprigs. Season the chicken all over with salt and pepper.

Scatter the 16 lemon wedges in roasting pan and place a rosemary sprig in center. Place chicken, breast down, over rosemary and lemons. Squeeze juice of remaining half lemon over chicken, and drizzle lightly with olive oil. Place in the oven and bake 20 minutes. Then bake 20 minutes longer on each side. To finish, turn chicken, breast-side up, and bake 10 to 15 minutes longer, until skin is brown and crisp, and juices run clear when tipped. (Baste with additional olive oil or pan juices each time the chicken is turned.) Let rest 10 minutes, carve, and serve.

SERVES 4

PEPPERED TUNA
WITH OLIVES AND LEMON

This 10-minute entrée is special enough to serve at an elegant dinner party.

    4 small tuna steaks
    coarse salt
    1 tablespoon plus 1 teaspoon cracked black
        pepper
    1/3 cup plus 2 tablespoons olive oil
    1/4 cup Kalamata olives, pitted and chopped
    1/2 teaspoon grated lemon zest

Season the tuna all over with salt. Divide the pepper into four parts and generously coat both sides of each piece with pepper.

Preheat the oven to 200 degrees F.

Heat 1 tablespoon of oil in a large skillet over high heat. Sear the fish, two pieces at a time, 2 minutes per side, adding 1 tablespoon or so of oil between batches. Transfer finished pieces to ovenproof platter in oven.

Meanwhile place a small skillet over medium-high heat and pour in the remaining ⅓ cup of olive oil. Add the olives and lemon zest, and cook, swirling the pan, just to heat through, less than 1 minute. Pour the hot oil over the fish, and serve.

SERVES 4

"Once we have known the taste of a lemon we never forget it and are liable to salivate at the very sight of anyone sucking one."

    —*Margaret Visser from* Much Depends on Dinner

PORK TENDERLOIN
WITH LEMON CAPER SAUCE

Tenderloins cook quickly and serve up elegantly in this lovely spin on scallopini.

4 garlic cloves, minced
2 tablespoons chopped fresh rosemary
1 tablespoon grated lemon zest
2 teaspoons coarse salt
2 teaspoons coarsely ground pepper
2 pork tenderloins, about ¾ pound each
2 tablespoons olive oil
½ cup beef broth
½ cup lemon juice
¼ stick butter, cut in 4 pieces
1 tablespoon capers

Preheat oven to 450 degrees F.

Combine garlic, rosemary, lemon zest, salt, and pepper. Divide in two and press mixture evenly all over meat. In large ovenproof skillet, warm oil over medium heat. Add meat and cook, turning until evenly browned, 8 to 10 minutes. Transfer to oven. Roast 15 to 20 minutes, or until done to taste. Remove pork from pan and keep warm.

Set pan over high heat and stir in broth and lemon juice, scraping up browned bits. Bring to a boil, and cook until reduced by a third. Whisk in butter, one piece at a time. Stir in capers. Cut pork into thick slices and serve topped with sauce.

SERVES 4 TO 6

SEAFOOD RISOTTO

Serve this rich risotto as a main course with a simple salad, some bread, and a good, cold white wine.

3/4 stick butter
1 onion, diced
3 garlic cloves, minced
6 plum tomatoes, peeled, seeded, and roughly
    chopped
1/4 cup chopped fresh Italian parsley
2 tablespoons chopped fresh basil
2 cups Arborio *or* medium-grain rice
1/2 cup lemon juice
2 tablespoons grated lemon zest
4 cups fish stock *or* reduced-sodium chicken
    broth, heated
1/2 pound medium shrimp, peeled and deveined
1/2 pound bay scallops
1 dozen mussels, scrubbed
1 dozen clams, scrubbed
salt and pepper

Melt the butter in large, heavy saucepan over medium heat. Sauté onion until translucent, about 5 minutes. Stir in garlic and cook 30 seconds longer. Add tomatoes, half of the parsley, and basil. Cook, stirring frequently, 10 minutes. Stir in rice, reduce heat to low, and cook, stirring constantly, until all liquid is absorbed, about 5 minutes. Add the lemon juice and zest, and cook, stirring constantly, until completely absorbed.

Add 3 cups hot stock, 1 cup at a time, stirring constantly after each addition, until liquid is absorbed. Just before adding final cup of stock, stir in shrimp and scallops. Stir in last cup of stock. When liquid has nearly all been absorbed, add mussels and clams. Cover and simmer until shells open, discarding any unopened shells. Sprinkle with remaining parsley and serve immediately.

SERVES 4 TO 6

STEAMED SEA BASS
WITH LEMONS AND OREGANO

Who says low fat has to feel dowdy? Here's a sophisticated way to highlight the fish's flavor without overpowering it with sauce.

4 garlic cloves, crushed
1 tablespoon salt
1 teaspoon peppercorns
2 lemons, thinly sliced
4 sea bass fillets, about 6 ounces each
olive oil for coating
salt and pepper
1 tablespoon chopped fresh oregano

The Parts of a Lemon

Lemon skin is composed of two parts—the bright yellow zest that holds aromatic oils, and the cottony, white pith beneath that cushions the juicy fruit. Though the bitter pith is not used in cooking, it has industrial uses. Pectin, used to solidify jams, comes from the pith.

Fill the bottom of a steamer or large saucepan one-third full with water. Add garlic, salt, and peppercorns, and bring to simmer.

Line steamer rack with half the lemon slices. Lightly coat fish with olive oil, and season to taste with salt and pepper. Arrange fish over the lemons. Place remaining lemons over the fish. Scatter oregano over the top. Cover pan and steam 10 minutes, or until fish is almost cooked through. Serve hot, garnished with lemon slices.

SERVES 4

Lemon leaves, sometimes attached to the fruit in ethnic markets, are lovely for decorating and also can be used whole in marinades and to protect and impart flavor to fish on the grill. Citric acid, from lemons, is the most commonly used acid in commercial food preserving and curing.

GRILLED CRAB LEGS
WITH LEMON VINAIGRETTE

*King crab legs, available precooked and frozen in
the seafood section at the supermarket, are a great
summertime treat.*

4 Alaskan king crab legs, thawed, cracked,
   and split
olive oil for brushing
2 bunches watercress, trimmed, washed, and
   cut in 2-inch lengths
6 tablespoons olive oil
6 tablespoons lemon juice
2 garlic cloves
salt and freshly ground pepper

Preheat the broiler or grill.

Arrange crab legs in a single layer on tray,
and lightly brush with olive oil. Broil or grill
about 3 minutes, turning once.

Meanwhile place the watercress in a bowl.
In another bowl, whisk together the olive oil,
lemon juice, garlic, salt, and pepper. Spoon

about 2 tablespoons of dressing on the salad and toss. Divide and place on four serving plates.

Transfer crab legs to a tray and drizzle with the remaining dressing. Top each salad with warm crab legs, and serve.

SERVES 4

How to Pick a Lemon

The best lemons are bright yellow, glossy, and feel heavy in the hand. Avoid lemons whose skins look dull and shriveled. Lemons will keep longer in the refrigerator, but we like them on the counter, purely for aesthetic reasons. Bring chilled lemons back to room temperature for maximum juice yield.

MOROCCAN LAMB STEW WITH PRESERVED LEMONS

This exotic stew is a melange of sweet, sour, salty, and spicy. Preserved lemons, a Moroccan condiment, are available in gourmet and Middle Eastern markets, as is harissa.

3 pounds lamb shoulder, cut in large cubes
    with bone
salt and freshly ground pepper
4 tablespoons olive oil
2 onions, chopped
3 carrots, peeled and sliced on the diagonal
3 garlic cloves, minced
½-inch length fresh ginger, peeled and grated
½ teaspoon crushed saffron threads
½ teaspoon turmeric
⅛ teaspoon ground cinnamon
1 quart chicken stock
2 cups pitted prunes (1 12-ounce package)
1 to 2 quarters "Preserved Lemons" (see p. 52)
couscous or rice for serving

HARISSA PASTE

- ¼ cup chopped fresh cilantro
- 2 teaspoons lemon juice
- 2 tablespoons olive oil
- 2 teaspoons harissa

Season the lamb all over with salt and pepper. Heat 2 tablespoons of the oil in a large, heavy Dutch oven over high heat. Sear meat in batches until evenly browned. Transfer meat to a platter.

Add remaining oil to pan over medium-high heat. Sauté the onions about 5 minutes. Add carrots and cook, stirring occasionally, about 10 minutes longer, to soften. Turn up heat, and add garlic and ginger. Cook 1 minute. Stir in saffron, turmeric, and cinnamon. Pour in stock to cover (adding water if necessary), and bring nearly to a boil. Cover, reduce to a simmer, and cook about 1 hour, until meat is tender. Skim and discard foam occasionally.

Taste sauce and adjust with salt and pepper. Stir in prunes and cook, covered, 20 minutes longer. (If making in advance, the stew may be frozen.) Dice the preserved lemons and stir them into the stew.

To serve, make the (optional) harissa. Mix together the ingredients in a small bowl. Serve stew over rice or couscous. Pass harissa in small bowl for guests to add to taste.

SERVES 4 TO 6

SPRIGHTLY SIDES
AND
SPREADS

LEMON PARSLEY BASMATI RICE

This rice is subtly flavored so it goes well with just about anything—grilled or stir-fried chicken, fish, or the vegetable of your choice.

1 cup basmati rice, rinsed 3 times
1¼ cups chicken stock
2 garlic cloves, peeled and crushed
grated zest of 1 lemon
1 teaspoon salt
freshly ground pepper to taste
3 tablespoons freshly chopped Italian parsley

Place the rice in a medium saucepan with the chicken stock, garlic, lemon, salt, and pepper. Bring to a boil, reduce to a simmer, and cover. Cook about 18 minutes for firm, dry rice. Stir in the parsley, and cover again. Let sit 10 minutes. Fluff with a fork and serve.

SERVES 4

Since lemon juice plays such a large role in cooking, several options exist for efficient lemon-squeezing. For large quantities, we like an electric citrus squeezer. Simple glass or ceramic squeezers available at the hardware store are good for just a few lemons at a time. (We keep a small strainer handy for the seeds.) And last, but never least, is the quick hand method favored by restaurant chefs. Simply roll the lemon on the counter, leaning down with your weight to loosen juice sacs. Cut in half across width, pierce with a fork in the center, and twist to extract juice. Juice may be stored in a sealed container in the refrigerator for about a week. Shake before using. The juice of one lemon equals about four tablespoons.

COLD ARTICHOKES WITH DOUBLE-LEMON MAYONNAISE

Need we say more? Artichokes and mayo were made for each other.

   1 lemon, halved
   3 garlic cloves, crushed and peeled
   2½ teaspoons salt
   1 teaspoon peppercorns
   1 bay leaf
   2 to 3 large artichokes
   2 egg yolks
   2 tablespoons lemon juice
   1 teaspoon dry mustard
   1¼ cups olive oil
   1 to 2 teaspoons grated lemon zest
   capers (optional)

Fill large pot three-quarters full of water. Add lemon, garlic, 2 teaspoons salt, peppercorns, and bay leaf. Bring to a boil.

Meanwhile, trim artichoke stems. Remove and discard bottom leaves. Cut about 1 inch off tops and snip prickly ends of outer leaves with scissors. Plunge artichokes into boiling water, cover, and boil gently 30 to 40 minutes, until outer leaves are easily pulled off. Drain upside down and chill.

In food processor or blender, process egg yolks, lemon juice, mustard, and ½ teaspoon salt. With machine running, slowly add oil in a steady stream. Add lemon zest and pulse to blend. Transfer to small bowl and sprinkle with capers, if desired. Serve with chilled artichokes for dipping.

SERVES 4 TO 6

PRESERVED LEMONS

These pickled lemons nicely accent meat, fish, or chicken. Use for "Moroccan Lamb Stew with Preserved Lemons" (see page 44) or to perk up grilled fish or roasted chicken.

3 to 4 large lemons
$1/2$ cup coarse salt
2 bay leaves
1 teaspoon peppercorns
3 small dried red peppers
1 to $1 1/2$ cups lemon juice

Scrub the lemons with liquid soap and water. Rinse well and cut in quarters lengthwise. Place on a plate, cover loosely with plastic wrap, and microwave at high power 1 minute.

Meanwhile in a small bowl, mix together salt, bay leaves, peppercorns, and red peppers.

Cut lemon pieces in half again lengthwise. Place a layer in the bottom of a 1-quart glass jar. Sprinkle in salt mixture and keep repeating layers, tamping down with a spoon, until jar is full. Add lemon juice to fill. Cover tightly and shake to distribute spices. Marinate in the refrigerator 10 to 14 days, shaking the jar daily.

To serve, remove lemon wedges, and rinse. Dice to use as a condiment. Or serve over grilled fish, or thinly sliced and stuffed under the skin of roasted chicken. Store in a sealed container in the refrigerator up to 1 year.

LEMON MARMALADE

All it takes is lemons and lots of sugar to make the most sublime marmalade.

4 cups thinly sliced lemons (about 6 whole
lemons)
5½ cups sugar

In large bowl, combine lemon slices and 7 cups water. Cover and let stand 24 hours. Drain.

In large saucepan, combine lemon slices and 7 cups fresh water. Bring to a boil and cook rapidly 25 minutes, stirring occasionally. Stir in sugar. When mixture returns to boil, cook, stirring frequently, until thermometer registers 220 degrees F, about 30 minutes. Skim off foam and pour into hot, sterilized ½-pint jars to within ½ inch of top. Wipe rims clean, and seal with lids and screw bands. Place jars in large pan with water to cover. Boil for 10 minutes. Cool and store in a cool place.

MAKES 7 (½-PINT) JARS

LEMON OLIVE OIL

Lemon-infused oil makes a great instant dressing for vegetables, grilled meats, fish, and bread. Store in a beautiful bottle for gift-giving.

5 lemons
1½ cups olive oil
strip of lemon zest (optional)

Slice lemons, and finely chop, including peel. Transfer to a bowl and add oil. Let stand overnight.

Set strainer lined with two layers of cheese-cloth over the bowl. Pour oil through strainer. Gather up cheesecloth, and squeeze to extract as much oil as possible. Let stand until oil and lemon juice have separated.

Spoon off oil into a jar or bottle or carefully draw oil into turkey baster and transfer to a bottle. Discard lemon juice. Add length of lemon zest, if desired, and seal. Store in refrigerator.

MAKES 1½ CUPS

Lemon trees are subtropical evergreens that thrive in warm, dry climates like those of California and southern Italy. Too much rain spoils the fruit—the reason they don't do well in Florida. Lemon trees prefer their water at the root.

The trees bear fruit year round with a yearly pruning. To turn from green to yellow, lemons need cool air. On commercial farms, lemons are picked green, washed, scrubbed, and turned yellow off the tree by curing with ethylene gas—the same gas emitted by ripening bananas. The lemons are then placed in storage at 58 degrees F for three to six months. Before the lemons go to market, their skins are first treated with fungicides and then waxed to replace their original shine.

LEMONY CAKES, COOKIES, AND OTHER BAKED GOODS

SHAKER LEMON PIE

Traditional Southern Shaker pie contains whole citrus slices macerated in sugar to a tender translucency and then baked. The resulting pie is exceptionally sour.

3 large lemons
2 cups sugar
¼ teaspoon salt
2 frozen pie crusts, defrosted
4 eggs, lightly beaten
½ stick butter, melted
3 tablespoons all-purpose flour
milk and sugar for glazing

Slice lemons paper thin, discarding ends and seeds. Toss lemons, sugar, and salt together in large bowl. Cover and marinate 12 to 24 hours at room temperature, tossing occasionally until lemons are translucent.

On a floured board, lightly roll out one piece of dough to a 12-inch circle and line a 9-inch pie pan. Roll remaining dough to a 12-inch circle. Chill both.

Preheat oven to 425 degrees F.

Whisk eggs with butter and flour. Add lemons and transfer to lined pie plate, smoothing the top. Cover with top crust, trim edges, and crimp. Cut steam vents in top crust. Brush lightly with milk and sprinkle with sugar for glaze. Bake $\frac{1}{2}$ hour. Reduce heat to 350 degrees F and bake until crust is golden, 20 to 30 minutes longer. Cool completely. Refrigerate if not serving immediately. Return pie to room temperature before serving.

MAKES 1 PIE

LEMON TART

*Served cold, this elegant French tart is a favorite
summer dessert.*

  1 prepared tart crust
  6 tablespoons butter, softened
  ²/₃ cup sugar
  3 eggs
  ¼ cup heavy cream
  grated zest and juice of 3 lemons

Preheat oven to 425 degrees F.

On a lightly floured board, roll out dough
and line a 10-inch tart pan. Chill 15 minutes.

Line the crust with aluminum foil, and prick
a few times with a fork. Fill with weights such as
dried beans or uncooked rice, and bake 15 minutes. Remove from oven and remove weights.
Reduce oven to 325 degrees F.

In a large bowl, with mixer beat together the
butter and sugar until light. Beat in the eggs and
cream. Then beat in the lemon zest and juice.
(Do not worry about curdling.) Pour into pre-

baked shell. Bake about 1 hour, until crust is golden and top begins to brown. Cool on a rack and chill in refrigerator.

MAKES 1

Lemon Varieties

There are three types of lemon: common, rough, and sweet. The lemons we get in the market are common, egg-shaped Eurekas in the summer and Lisbons in the fall. Rough lemons are used as rootstock for other citrus. Sweet lemons are not really sweet, just less acidic. Meyer lemons, the small, round, thin-skinned variety favored by gourmets, are considered sweet lemons. Look for them in specialty markets and on backyard trees.

LEMON POPPY SEED MUFFINS

These moist, fluffy, little seed cakes get an extra dose of lemon, first in the seeds and then in the batter. They are well worth the extra work.

$\frac{1}{2}$ cup poppy seeds
2 tablespoons honey
2 tablespoons water
3 tablespoons lemon juice
1 stick butter, softened
$\frac{1}{2}$ cup sugar
2 eggs
1 tablespoon grated lemon zest
$\frac{3}{4}$ cup plain yogurt
$1\frac{3}{4}$ cups all-purpose flour
1 teaspoon baking soda
2 teaspoons baking powder
$\frac{1}{2}$ teaspoon salt

Combine poppy seeds, honey, and water in small saucepan and place over medium heat. Cook, stirring frequently, until seeds are evenly moistened, about 4 minutes. Cool and then stir in lemon juice.

Preheat oven to 375 degrees F. Grease muffin tins or line with paper cups.

In large mixing bowl, cream butter and sugar until smooth. Beat in eggs, zest, and yogurt. Add seed mixture and combine.

In another bowl, combine flour, baking soda, baking powder, and salt. Add dry ingredients to liquid and stir until combined. Fill muffin cups to top. Bake about 20 minutes, until tops are golden and center is done when tested.

Makes 12

LEMONADE WAFERS

If you believe as we do that a cookie can never be too thin, too rich, or too sour, you'll adore these delicate iced wafers.

1 stick butter, softened
²/₃ cup sugar
1 egg yolk
1 tablespoon grated lemon zest
1 teaspoon vanilla
¹/₂ cup all-purpose flour
¹/₂ cup plus 2 tablespoons cake flour
¹/₂ teaspoon salt

GLAZE

³/₄ cup confectioners' sugar
1 tablespoon plus 1 teaspoon lemon juice
1 teaspoon grated lemon zest

Cream together butter and sugar until light and fluffy. Beat in egg yolk, zest, and vanilla.

In another bowl, combine two flours and salt. Add the butter and gently beat until flour disappears and dough holds together. Remove, press into a ball, and divide in two. Handling lightly, on a floured board, form each piece into small log, about 1½ x 4 inches. Wrap each in plastic and chill up to 1 week.

To bake, preheat oven to 375 degrees F. Lightly grease two cookie sheets and line with parchment paper, if desired. Cut each log across width into ⅜-inch slices. Arrange slices on cookie sheet, 1 inch apart. Bake about 10 minutes, until edges are golden and centers set. Transfer to racks to cool.

For glaze, in a small bowl whisk together sugar, lemon juice, and zest until smooth and thick enough to spread. (Thin with a few drops of lemon juice or thicken with sugar, as necessary.)

Hold each cookie along the edge and spread a thin layer of glaze with a small spatula or butter knife. Dry and store in a cookie tin.

MAKES 30

LEMON BARS

For a pure lemon hit, classic lemon bars are hard to beat. Whip up a batch for your next barbecue or bake sale, and watch them disappear almost as quickly as you made them.

CRUST

1¼ cups all-purpose flour
¼ cup confectioners' sugar
1 stick butter, softened
½ teaspoon grated lemon zest

FILLING

3 eggs
1 cup sugar
½ cup lemon juice
1 tablespoon grated lemon zest
2 tablespoons all-purpose flour
½ teaspoon baking powder
confectioners' sugar for dusting

Preheat oven to 350 degrees F.

For crust, combine flour and sugar in mixing bowl. Cut butter into tablespoon-size pieces and add to flour, along with zest. Blend with fingers or pastry blender until dough holds together when pressed. Press evenly into 8-inch-square baking pan. Bake about 20 minutes, until edges are golden and sides start to pull away from pan. Cool on rack 5 minutes. Reduce oven to 325 degrees F.

For filling, lightly whisk eggs in a bowl. Whisk in sugar, lemon juice, and zest. Stir in flour and baking powder. Pour over baked crust and return to oven. Bake 25 minutes, until top is set when pressed in center. Cool on rack. Dust with confectioners' sugar and cut into squares. Store in the refrigerator.

MAKES 20

LEMON SPONGE CAKE

A simple sponge cake is the building block for a wide variety of layered cakes. An electric mixer is your best bet for beating in the necessary volume.

4 eggs
½ cup sugar
2 teaspoons grated lemon zest
¾ cup cake flour, sifted
2 tablespoons butter, melted

Preheat the oven to 350 degrees F. Butter the bottom and sides of a 9-inch round cake pan. Line with parchment paper and dust all over with flour.

Combine the eggs and sugar in a large stainless-steel mixing bowl. Place directly over medium-low burner and gently whisk until pale, smooth, and foamy.

Pour into the bowl of an electric mixer and add lemon zest. Whisk at high speed several minutes, until the batter is thick, pale, and more than doubled in volume. Sift the flour again, into the batter. Gently fold until the flour just disappears.

Pour about one-third of the batter into a small mixing bowl. Pour in the melted butter, fold three or four times, and pour back into the larger mixing bowl. Fold to blend and pour into prepared pan, smoothing the top. Gently tap on the counter to remove air.

Bake about 35 minutes until the center springs back when pressed and the top is golden. Cool in pan on rack. Then invert onto rack and peel paper off.

Serve plain with whipped cream or gussy it up. For an easy party cake, prepare the "Candied Lemon Slices" (see page 76) and 2 cups sweetened whipped cream. Pierce cooled cake all over with a skewer or toothpick, and brush with syrup from candied lemons. Spread the top and sides with whipped cream, and decorate top with lemon slice halves.

To really outdo yourself, prepare the "Lemon Curd" (see page 82) and 2 cups unsweetened whipped cream. Split the cooled cake in half horizontally, and fill the center with a layer of lemon curd. Fold the remaining lemon curd into the whipped cream, and coat the top and sides of the cake. Refrigerate to set. Decorate the top with "Candied Lemon Slices" (see page 76).

SERVES 6 TO 8

LEMON PECAN TEA BREAD

This sunny lemon loaf is a wonderful way to perk up winter appetites.

1 stick butter, room temperature
1 cup sugar
2 eggs, lightly beaten
1½ cups all-purpose flour
½ teaspoon baking powder
½ teaspoon baking soda
½ teaspoon salt
½ teaspoon vanilla
2½ teaspoons grated lemon zest
½ cup plus 1 tablespoon lemon juice
¾ cup finely chopped pecans
¾ cup confectioners' sugar
pecan halves for decorating

Preheat oven to 350 degrees F. Grease and flour 9 x 5 x 3-inch loaf pan.

Beat butter in a large mixing bowl until smooth. Gradually add sugar, beating until light. Beat in eggs.

In a separate bowl, sift together flour, baking powder, baking soda, and salt. Sprinkle about half of flour mixture over butter mixture and gently beat until blended.

In a separate bowl, combine vanilla, 2 teaspoons lemon zest, and ½ cup juice. Beat half of liquid mixture into batter. Add remaining dry ingredients and liquid and beat into batter to blend well. Stir in chopped nuts.

Pour into prepared pan. Bake about 45 minutes or until toothpick inserted in center comes out clean. Cool in the pan on a rack 10 minutes, then turn bread out and cool completely.

In a small bowl, combine powdered sugar with remaining tablespoon lemon juice and ½ teaspoon zest. Stir until smooth. Pour over cooled loaf. Decorate top with pecan halves.

MAKES 1 LOAF

LEMON WAFFLES
WITH RASPBERRY SAUCE

What better reason to get out of bed in the morning than lemony yellow waffles with bright red berry sauce?

2 cups all-purpose flour
2 teaspoons baking powder
$\frac{1}{2}$ teaspoon baking soda
$\frac{1}{2}$ teaspoon salt
$\frac{1}{4}$ cup sugar
$1\frac{1}{2}$ cups buttermilk
3 eggs
grated zest of 2 lemons
$\frac{1}{4}$ cup lemon juice
1 stick butter, melted
Raspberry Sauce

Preheat waffle iron.

In a large mixing bowl, combine flour, baking powder, baking soda, salt, and sugar.

In another bowl, whisk together buttermilk, eggs, lemon zest, and juice. Add butter, and whisk until smooth. Add liquid ingredients to flour mixture and stir just to combine.

Pour onto the waffle maker and follow manufacturer's instructions. Serve with Raspberry Sauce or warm maple syrup.

MAKES 8

RASPBERRY SAUCE

1 pint fresh raspberries or 1 (10-ounce) bag
    frozen raspberries
$1/3$ cup sugar

Combine raspberries and sugar in small saucepan and cook over low heat, stirring occasionally, about 5 minutes, until berries dissolve. Serve hot.

MAKES $1/2$ CUP

JUST DESSERTS

CANDIED LEMON SLICES

Lovely, translucent lemon slices can be made in advance and used to decorate "Lemon Sponge Cake" (see page 68), lemon curd tarts, or lemony quick-breads or muffins. They send an instant sweet-and-sour message to the brain.

1 lemon, sliced paper thin with serrated blade
½ cup water
1 cup sugar
sugar for dusting (optional)

Combine the ingredients in a small, heavy saucepan over moderate heat. Bring to a simmer, and cook at low heat 20 to 25 minutes, until skins are soft. Set aside to cool. Lemon slices can be reserved in their syrup in a covered container in the refrigerator as long as a week.

To use, with tongs transfer lemon slices to paper towels to drain. Then transfer lemon slices to a plate and dust all over with optional sugar or simply arrange as desired on the baked item.

ENOUGH FOR 2 CAKES

- *Streak hair*
- *Lighten the skin and remove freckles*
- *Clean and deodorize a cutting board*
- *Clean brass, copper, and stainless steel with a paste of lemon juice and salt*
- *Clean wooden furniture*
- *Soothe the rash of poison ivy*
- *Prevent cut fruits and vegetables from browning*

LEMON THYME GRANITA

The perfect hot-weather snack. For a special presentation, serve inside of hollowed-out lemon halves.

2 cups water
$\frac{1}{2}$ cup sugar
$1\frac{1}{2}$ teaspoons finely grated lemon zest
2 sprigs thyme
$\frac{1}{2}$ cup lemon juice
additional thyme sprigs for garnish

Combine the water, sugar, lemon zest, and two thyme sprigs in small saucepan. Bring to a boil, reduce to a simmer, and cook, stirring frequently, until transparent. Cool and remove thyme.

Pour into round metal cake pan, add lemon juice, and stir. Place in the freezer and freeze until solid, 3 to 6 hours. Remove and let sit 5 minutes to soften. Break into chunks with a blunt knife, and transfer to a food processor fitted with a metal blade. Pulse until a granular slush is formed.

Or by hand, freeze mixture about 1 hour, until crystals are formed along the sides. Remove, and with a fork, stir, breaking and combining the hardened ice with the liquid. Repeat this procedure every 15 minutes until a slush is formed. Store in the freezer up to 1 day. Garnish with thyme sprigs.

SERVES 6

The California Lemon

California produces 80 percent of the lemons sold in America—thanks to Father Junipero Serra, who started cultivating lemon groves at the San Diego mission in 1796.

LEMON ICE CREAM

We like to make homemade ice cream with lemons since it is a difficult flavor to find in commercial brands.

4 lemons
3/4 cup heavy cream
1 cup half-and-half
4 egg yolks
1/2 cup sugar
1 teaspoon vanilla

Wash the lemons well and grate all the zest. Squeeze the juice of two lemons.

Combine cream, half-and-half, and lemon zest in heavy saucepan. Bring to a boil.

In a large bowl, whisk together egg yolks and sugar until pale and thick. Pour in hot cream mixture, stirring constantly until combined and smooth. Stir in lemon juice and vanilla. Strain into another bowl and chill. When cold, pour into ice cream maker and follow manufacturer's instructions. Store in a sealed container in the freezer.

MAKES 1½ PINTS

LEMON CURD

This rich yellow custard is perfect for filling pre-baked tart shells or spreading on raisin scones at afternoon tea. Also use it as a cake filling for "Lemon Sponge Cake" (see page 68). Homemade curd is infinitely better than the stuff sold in stores.

3 eggs
¾ cup sugar
1 tablespoon finely grated lemon zest
1 cup lemon juice
4 tablespoons butter, cold, cut in tablespoon-
    size pieces

In bowl or top of double boiler, whisk eggs until smooth. Whisk in sugar, zest, and lemon juice. Place over small pan of simmering water and cook over low heat, stirring constantly with a wooden spoon until thick and pale yellow, 7 to 10 minutes. Stir in butter, 1 tablespoon at a time, until thoroughly combined and smooth. Set bowl over ice, stirring frequently, to cool. Cover with plastic wrap, and store in the refrigerator up to 5 days.

MAKES 1½ CUPS

The Lemonade Trail

Citrus limon, *or the cultivated lemon, originated in the Indus Valley of India's Fertile Crescent. From there they migrated to China and Malaysia and reached the Mediterranean region during the Crusades. The Normans brought them to Sicily. Columbus carried citrus seeds to the New World, where today half of the world's crop is grown in California.*

LEMON CURD RIPPLE ICE CREAM

A match made in heaven: vanilla ice cream and tangy lemon curd!

- 4 egg yolks
- 3 cups heavy cream
- 1 cup milk
- 1 cup sugar
- 2 teaspoons vanilla
- 1 cup "Lemon Curd" (see page 82)

In a large bowl, whisk egg yolks until slightly thickened. Set aside.

In saucepan, combine cream, milk, and sugar. Bring to a gentle boil over medium-high heat, stirring to dissolve sugar. Reduce heat to low. Whisk about 1 cup hot mixture into the yolks, then whisk yolk mixture back into the pan. Cook, stirring constantly, until mixture is thick enough to coat the back of spoon. Stir in vanilla. Pour through a fine sieve into a large bowl. Cool slightly, then cover, and refrigerate at least 4 hours or overnight.

Freeze in ice cream maker according to manufacturer's instructions. Transfer ice cream to a freezer container and gently stir in "Lemon Curd" just until marbleized. Cover tightly and freeze at least 2 hours before serving.

MAKES 1½ QUARTS

LEMON PUDDING CUPS

Dress up these lovely little puddings with chocolate shavings or a few raspberries scattered over the top.

¼ cup all-purpose flour
¾ cup sugar
¼ teaspoon salt
1 cup heavy cream
3 eggs, separated
⅓ cup lemon juice
1 tablespoon grated lemon zest

Preheat oven to 350 degrees F. Butter 6 (6-ounce) custard cups or individual ramekins.

In a small bowl, combine flour, sugar, and salt.

In large bowl, whisk cream with egg yolks, lemon juice, and zest. Gradually whisk in dry ingredients to blend.

In another mixer bowl, beat egg whites until stiff but not dry. Gently fold into batter. Pour into prepared dishes, and set in a large roasting pan. Place on oven rack and pour enough water into the roasting pan to come halfway up the sides of the dishes. Bake until puddings are deep golden on top, about 40 minutes. Serve warm, or cool to room temperature.

SERVES 6

"A modern kitchen without a lemon in it is gravely ill-equipped."

—*Margaret Visser from* Much Depends on Dinner

ICED LEMON DROPS

Is it a summer drink or is it a cool dessert? Either way, this frosted treat is sure to quicken sleepy pulses on a hot summer evening.

    2 lemon wedges
    sugar for dipping
    1 cup lemon sorbet
    2 tablespoons vodka
    4 tablespoons lemon juice
    2 thin lemon slices

Moisten the rims of two martini glasses with a lemon wedge. Spread a thin layer of sugar on a plate, and dip each glass to coat rim with sugar.

Scoop ½ cup of sorbet in each glass. Top each with 1 tablespoon of vodka and 2 tablespoons of lemon juice. Top with a lemon slice on the rim and serve.

SERVES 2

PUCKERING DRINKS

ICED LEMON GINGER TEA

This favorite was taught to us by chefs Mary Sue Milliken and Susan Feniger.

1 quart water
juice of 2 lemons (reserve the rinds)
2 tablespoons freshly grated ginger
3 tablespoons honey
thinly sliced lemons for garnish

Bring the water to a boil. Add the lemon juice, squeezed lemons, and ginger. Let steep about 20 minutes. Stir in honey. Strain into a pitcher and chill. Serve in iced glasses topped with thin lemon slices.

MAKES 1 QUART

LEMONADE

For limeade, substitute lime juice or mix half lemon/half lime.

3/4 cup sugar
7 1/2 cups water
3/4 cup lemon juice
1 lemon, washed and thinly sliced

Combine the sugar with 3/4 cup of the water in a small saucepan. Cook at a low boil, stirring occasionally, until the liquid is clear, about 3 minutes.

Pour into a pitcher, and stir in the lemon juice, remaining water, and lemon slices. Refrigerate and serve over ice.

MAKES 1 1/2 QUARTS

SPICED LEMON BRANDY

Serve this iced, spiced brandy at the end of a summer barbecue.

1 lemon
1 cinnamon stick
½ teaspoon whole cloves
3 allspice berries
2 cups brandy
⅔ cup sugar
lemon twists

With vegetable peeler, remove lemon zest in continuous spiral. Place zest, cinnamon, cloves, and allspice in jar. Add brandy. Cover tightly and let stand 1 week, shaking jar occasionally. Remove zest and spices and stir in sugar. Cover again and let stand 1 week longer. Serve over crushed ice with lemon twists.

MAKES ABOUT 2 CUPS

LEMONY GIN JULEP

You don't have to be from the South to appreciate the restorative qualities of an icy sweet-sour julep on a sweltering day.

3 tablespoons lemon juice
$\frac{1}{4}$ teaspoon finely grated lemon zest
2 mint sprigs
2 tablespoons sugar
$\frac{1}{4}$ cup gin
crushed ice
club soda
lemon twist and mint sprigs for garnish

In a tall glass, stir lemon juice, zest, mint sprigs, and sugar, bruising mint with spoon. Stir in gin. Fill glass almost to top with ice. Pour in soda to top. Garnish with lemon twist and additional mint, and sip.

MAKES 1

HOT MAPLE LEMON GROG

For your next pirate party!

1 shot dark rum
2 tablespoons lemon juice
1 to 2 teaspoons maple syrup
1 cup hot tea
lemon slices
cinnamon stick for stirring (optional)

In a mug, stir together rum, lemon juice, and maple syrup. Pour in hot tea, top with lemon slices and optional cinnamon stick. Let steep a few minutes. Drink hot.

SERVES 1

Since the late 15th century, lemon juice has been recognized as an excellent source of vitamin C. When the British navy was plagued by an epidemic of scurvy (a disease of the gums caused by vitamin C deficiency), lemon juice saved the day. A dose of lemon juice was issued daily to each sailor after the fifth week at sea. In order to help get it down, the inventive sailors mixed the juice with their daily dose of rum and called it "grog." For the same reason, the British sailors ate another citrus fruit, the lime. Many people believe this is where the expression "limeys" came from when referring to the British.

Now vitamin C is recognized as an important agent in fighting colds. Even dyed-in-the-wool coffee drinkers will switch to hot tea with honey and lemon when trying to soothe a scratchy throat. Vitamin C also helps the body absorb iron and calcium.

CONVERSIONS

LIQUID
1 Tbsp = 15 ml
½ cup = 4 fl oz = 125 ml
1 cup = 8 fl oz = 250 ml

DRY
¼ cup = 4 Tbsp = 2 oz = 60 g
1 cup = ½ pound = 8 oz = 250 g

FLOUR
½ cup = 60 g
1 cup = 4 oz = 125 g

TEMPERATURE
400° F = 200° C = gas mark 6
375° F = 190° C = gas mark 5
350° F = 175° C = gas mark 4

MISCELLANEOUS
2 Tbsp butter = 1 oz = 30 g
1 inch = 2.5 cm
all-purpose flour = plain flour
baking soda = bicarbonate of soda
brown sugar = demerara sugar
heavy cream = double cream
sugar = caster sugar